CANAL HOUSE
COOKING

An Italian Summer

Hamilton & Hirsheimer

CANAL HOUSE
No. 6 Coryell Street
Lambertville, NJ 08530
thecanalhouse.com

ISBN 978-0-9827394-3-3

Printed in China

10 9 8 7 6 5 4 3 2 1

Book design by CANAL HOUSE, a group of artists who collaborate on design projects.
This book was designed by Melissa Hamilton, Christopher Hirsheimer & Teresa Hopkins.
Edited by Margo True & Copyedited by Valerie Saint-Rossy.
Editorial assistance by Julia Lee & Julie Sproesser.

With great appreciation to
Lori Di Mori & Jason Lowe for sharing their Tuscany
and to Jim Hirsheimer for sharing his iPhone image (page 3)

Canal House Cooking is home cooking by home cooks for home cooks. We use ingredients found in most markets. All the recipes are easy to prepare for the novice and experienced cook alike. We want to share them with you as fellow cooks along with our love of food and all its rituals. The everyday practice of simple cooking and the enjoyment of eating are two of the greatest pleasures in life.

CHRISTOPHER HIRSHEIMER served as food and design editor for *Metropolitan Home* magazine, and was one of the founders of *Saveur* magazine, where she was executive editor. She is a writer and a photographer.

MELISSA HAMILTON cofounded the restaurant Hamilton's Grill Room in Lambertville, New Jersey, where she served as executive chef. She worked at *Martha Stewart Living, Cook's Illustrated*, and at *Saveur* as food editor.

OUR WEBSITE

Our website, thecanalhouse.com, a companion to this book, offers our readers ways to get the best from supermarkets (what and how to buy, how to store it, cook it, and serve it). We'll tell you why a certain cut of meat works for a particular recipe; which boxes, cans, bottles, or tins are worthwhile; which apples are best for baking; and what to look for when buying olive oil, salt, or butter. We'll also suggest what's worth seeking out from specialty stores or mail-order sources, and why. And wait, there's more: We share our stories, the wines we are drinking, gardening tips, and events; and our favorite books, cooks, and restaurants are on our site. Take a look.

That's Amore!
Why We Love Italy 2

Rosato
Cin Cin! Drinking Pink Italian Style 6

Antipasti
Mozzarella in Carrozza 10, Caponata 11

Pizza, Riso & Pasta
Grilled Pizza 14, Raw Tomato Sauce 14
Hot Spaghetti Tossed with Raw Tomato Sauce 15, Rice Salad 17
Chickpeas Terra e Mare 18

Contorni
Roasted Onions Agrodolce 22, Grilled Tomatoes with Olive Oil & Oregano 23
Small Zucchini Poached in Olive Oil 23, Tomatoes with Tonnato Sauce 25
Swiss Chard with Capers & Currants 26, Romano Beans Stewed in Tomato Sauce 26

Pesce
Mixed Seafood Grill with Salmoriglio 30
Cold Poached Sea Bass & Lemon-Anchovy Mayonnaise 31
Salmon Carpaccio alla Harry's Bar 33

Carne
Grilled Steak with Bottarga Butter 36
Rolled Flank Steak with Pesto 39, A Pile of Grilled Lamb Chops Scottadito 40
Fried Rabbit & Fritto Misto of Herbs 43

Finale
Fig Gelato 46, Chilled Strawberries & Moscato d'Asti 47
Sweet Ricotta & Shaved Chocolate 47

Simplicity is the ultimate sophistication.—Leonardo da Vinci

We are very content to come to our studio every day—the lure of the big world doesn't quite have the pull that it used to. We have both traveled a lot in the past, our jobs required it, and in those days we loved nothing more than hopping on a plane to head off into the wild blue yonder. But it takes a lot to get us to leave home now—say, a lunch at Harry's Bar in Venice, or a day roaming around Rome, or the perfume of the famed white truffles of Piedmont shaved over fried eggs, or a slice of the famous Tuscan *bistecca alla fiorentina*, or eating gelato in sunny Palermo—actually, just about any meal in Italy. So off we went. We rented a house with a simple pretty kitchen, shopped in small town markets and cooked everything we found there. We rented a little car and drove all the backroads and ate our way up and down the boot! Now we'll share it all with you Casa Canale style. We are devoting our next three books to a year in Italy. This little booklet is an introduction to all the cooking that will follow! Its pages are filled with recipes like Grilled Pizza, Mozzarella in Carrozza, Caponata, Grilled Steak with Bottarga Butter, and Fig Gelato. We've kept it simple, it's summer!

Christopher & Melissa

Melissa and Christopher sussing out the streets of Florence

Rosato

From the top of the boot in the cool climate of the Alto Adige, down the Ligurian coast to sun-soaked Sicily, we found delicious rosatos for drinking pink Italiano style.

BRUCE NEYERS, Kermit Lynch Wine Merchant, Berkeley, CA

Punta Crena, Frizzante "Pettirosso" Rosato, Liguria, 2010
50% Sangiovese, 50% Rossese; The grapes grow high on hills that overlook the Ligurian coast where winemaking has been the Ruffino family business for more than 500 years. It tastes like Italy in a bottle. With its soft coral color and slight fizziness, it has a savory flavor that reminds us of a delicious tomato sauce—tart and acidic, vegetal and herby but with citrus fruit too. Really a fascinating bottle.

Sesti, Rosato, Tuscany, 2010
100% Sangiovese; The Sesti family began making this rosato because the family wanted something cooling to drink under the hot Tuscan sun. Now they produce about 400 cases, 100 of which come to the United States. It's soft and slightly effervescent with many layers of flavor. On the surface it is fresh and crisp, but underneath it has chewy fruit like dried apricots.

DARRELL CORTI, Corti Brothers, Sacramento, CA

Corte Gardoni, Bardolino Chiaretto, Veneto, 2010
50% Corvina, 30% Rondinella, 20% other grapes; The Piccoli family have vineyards planted among fruit orchards and olive trees. They make balsamic vinegar and olive oil, and began producing their own wine in 1971. Light pink, soft and with a nose full of peaches, it is exactly what you want from a rosato. Dreamy, perfumed, and perfectly balanced. It is one of only two rosati currently sold at Corti Brothers.

Proprietà Sperino, Rosa del Rosa, Piedmont, 2010
85% Nebbiolo, 10% Vespolina, 5% Croatina; Paolo De Marchi started making wine at his family's historic estate, the Castle of Lessona in via Sperino, where this rosato was born. First sip is like biting into a luscious piece of juicy, ripe fruit. It is tart with berries, fresh with citrus, and has good acidity for drinking with food.

LEVI DALTON, Sommelier, Bar Boulud, New York City

Montenidoli, Canaiuolo, Tuscany, 2010
100% Canaiuolo; This organic winery, in the hills north of Siena, sits on land that has been planted with vines since the time of the Crusades. Montenidoli means "mountain

of little nests" and refers to the chirping European Jays that are native to the area. This rosato has a beautiful, pale copper color and a distinct flavor of licorice on the finish. Its red fruit is subtle and its acidity is bright. It could almost be a white wine on taste alone.

Castello di Ama, Rosato, Tuscany, 2010
90% Sangiovese, 10% Merlot; This rosato has a red cherry color and gets its full body from Chianti Classico grapes. It is earthy and mushroomy and one of the biggest rosatos we tasted, but dry and drinkable too. It has substance at an excellent price.

JAMIE WOLFF, Chambers Street Wines, New York City

Fonterenza, Rosato, Tuscany, 2009
100% Sangiovese; Made by two dedicated sisters, Margherita and Francesca Padovani, who do all of the organic farming by hand. We were struck by the minerality of this wine. It smells like rocks in a cool stream and tastes like red berries.

Heinrich Mayr Nüsserhof, Lagrein Kretzer, Alto Adige, 2009
100% Lagrein; From the Bolzano Valley Basin, a warm sunny spot in the cool northern climate. The Nusser family has made wine from vines on this property since 1788. With a lovely fuchsia color, this wine tastes like raspberry jam, sour cherries, and strawberries. It has a nice long finish and is a bit peppery at the end.

NEAL ROSENTHAL, Rosenthal Wine Merchant

Bisson, Ciliegiolo, Rosé Golfo del Tigullio, Liguria, 2010
100% Ciliegiolo; From the Italian Rivieria, these grapes grow high on cliffs above the Ligurian coastline. Neal Rosenthal says he struggles to call this wine a rosé because of its intense bright fuchsia-red color, but it feels like a rosé through and through. It smells like delicious ripe cherries and has a lovely silkiness with no sharp edges. It is pretty and dry with good minerality.

CANAL HOUSE COOKING

Cantele, Negroamaro Rosato, Salento, 2010
100% Negroamaro; The Cantele family moved from northern Italy in the 1950s to make wine in Salento, the heel of the Italian boot, known as the "land of sun." Deliciously drinkable. It's great for easy afternoon sipping.

Tasca d'Almerita, Regaleali Le Rose, Sicily, 2010
100% Nerello Mascalese; From the massive Tasca d'Almerita estate known for its wines and its cooking school. This lovely rosato has a bright fresh quality.

antipasti

MOZZARELLA IN CARROZZA
makes 6

We eat these crisp little fried cheese sandwiches "in a carriage" as a snack at the end of the day with an aperitivo or cold glass of rosato (page 6). Just one to take the edge off our hunger or to whet our appetite. The sandwiches can be prepared ahead—assembled, breaded, and refrigerated—for a day or two before frying them. Finely crushed panko works as well as traditional dry bread crumbs for the outside coating.

½ cup flour
1 cup panko, finely crushed, or fine
   dry bread crumbs
2 eggs
12 slices thin white sandwich bread

6 slices fresh mozzarella,
   ¼ inch thick
6 anchovy filets, or 2 thin slices
   prosciutto, cut into thirds
Olive oil
Salt

Put the flour in a wide dish, put the panko in another wide dish, and beat the eggs in a third wide dish, and set them aside.

Lay out 6 slices of the bread on a cutting board. Place a slice of mozzarella on each piece of bread and lay an anchovy or slice of prosciutto on top. Finish each sandwich with another slice of bread. Press sandwiches firmly together. Using a large square or round cookie cutter (or just a sharp knife), cut the sandwiches into squares or circles, removing the crusts and encasing the cheese within the bread.

Working with one sandwich at a time, dredge it first in the flour, then moisten both sides and the edges in the eggs, then coat completely in the panko. Repeat with the remaining 5 sandwiches.

Add enough oil to a heavy large skillet to reach a depth of ½ inch. Heat the oil over medium heat until it is hot but not smoking (or until it reaches 350° on a candy thermometer). Working in batches, fry the sandwiches until they are golden brown on each side, 1–2 minutes per side. Use a slotted spatula to transfer the sandwiches to paper towels to drain. Sprinkle with a little salt.

Serve hot, but if that's not convenient, don't worry. They're still really good even when they've cooled off a bit.

CAPONATA
makes about 8 cups

We like to make this classic Sicilian eggplant antipasto sensuously chunky to take advantage of the eggplant's soft, silky texture and its affinity for big flavors—in this case, the delicious balance between sweet and sour. We make a generous batch, keep it in the fridge at the ready, and find ourselves serving it not only as an antipasto alongside slices of salumi, bruschetta, or hard-boiled eggs, but also spooned over grilled or poached fish and chicken, stirred hot or cold into pasta, and as an accompaniment to crispy fried rabbit (page 43) and chicken. It keeps for up to 1 week and the flavors improves as it sits.

2 large eggplants, cut into 1-inch cubes

¼ cup kosher salt

½ cup white wine vinegar

1 tablespoon sugar

¼ cup currants or raisins

¾ cup olive oil

3 ribs celery, cut into large dice

1 medium yellow onion, chopped

4 anchovy filets, chopped

One 28-ounce can whole peeled plum tomatoes, quartered, and their juices and the canning juices

1 cup large green olives, preferably Sicilian, pitted and halved

2 tablespoons capers

1 bay leaf

Pepper

Toss the eggplant with the salt in a colander and let the bitter liquid drain out for about 1 hour. Meanwhile, combine the vinegar and sugar in a small bowl. Add the currants and set aside to plump.

Pat the eggplant dry with paper towels. Heat ½ cup of the oil in a heavy wide pot over medium-high heat. Working in batches, fry eggplant until browned all over, about 10 minutes. Transfer eggplant with a slotted spatula to a bowl.

Add the remaining ¼ cup of oil, the celery, and the onions to the pot. Cook over medium heat until just soft, about 10 minutes. Stir in the anchovies. Add the tomatoes and the juices, olives, capers, and bay leaf. Return eggplant to the pot. Stir in the currants and vinegar. Simmer, gently stirring often, until the juices thicken a bit, 10–15 minutes. Season with pepper. Refrigerate for at least 1 day and up to 1 week. Remove bay leaf before serving.

Pizza, Riso & Pasta

GRILLED PIZZA
makes 6

It's too hot in the summer to be trapped indoors making pizza with the oven blasting away at 500°. Take it outside! Fire up a charcoal grill and make these smoky grilled flatbreads (an ancient method, after all).

FOR THE DOUGH
1 envelope (2¼ teaspoons) active
  dry yeast
3½ cups bread flour, plus more
  for dusting
6 tablespoons extra-virgin olive oil
½ cup semolina flour
1½ teaspoons salt

FOR THE RAW TOMATO SAUCE
1½–2 pounds ripe tomatoes

1–2 cloves garlic, finely chopped
½ cup passata di pomodoro, strained
  tomatoes, or tomato purée
4–6 tablespoons really good
  extra-virgin olive oil
Salt and pepper

TO ASSEMBLE
2 balls fresh mozzarella, sliced
Extra-virgin olive oil
Large handful small fresh basil leaves

For the dough, dissolve the yeast in ½ cup warm water in a medium bowl. Add ½ cup of the bread flour, stirring until the loose paste is smooth. Set aside until bubbly, 30–60 minutes. Stir in 1¼ cups warm water and 2 tablespoons of the olive oil. Put 1 tablespoon of oil into a large bowl and set aside.

Pulse the remaining 3 cups bread flour, the semolina flour, and salt together in the work bowl of a large food processor fitted with the steel blade. With the machine running, pour the yeast mixture in through the feed hole. A moist ball of dough will form. Process the dough for 1 minute. Transfer the dough to the large bowl with oil. Roll dough around in bowl until it is coated with oil. Cover the bowl with plastic wrap and let the dough rise in a warm spot until it has doubled in size, about 2 hours.

For the raw tomato sauce, grate a tomato on the large holes of a box grater into a large bowl, discarding the skin. Repeat until there are 2 cups of the loose tomato pulp. Add the garlic, passata, and oil, and season with salt and pepper. (This makes about 3 cups of sauce.)

Prepare a medium-hot hardwood charcoal or gas grill. Meanwhile, turn the dough out onto a well-floured work surface. Tear or cut the dough into sixths and shape each piece into a ball. Cover with a clean, damp, kitchen towel and let the dough relax for 5–30 minutes. Working with one ball at a time, roll the dough out with a rolling pin on the well-floured surface into a ½-inch-thick, free-form disc. Let the dough relax briefly, then roll it out further until it is about ¼ inch thick and about 12 inches in diameter. Slide the dough onto a floured pizza peel or rimless cookie sheet and prick all over with a fork.

Slide the dough onto the grill (don't worry, the dough will not seep through the grate) over the medium-hot coals and grill until the crust is set and the bottom has dark brown grill marks, about 30 seconds. Using long tongs, transfer crust to a clean surface, brush with some oil, and turn the grilled side up. Repeat rolling and grilling process with the remaining balls of dough.

To assemble and finish grilling the pizza, spoon a thin film of the prepared tomato sauce over each crust, cover with 4–6 slices of mozzarella, drizzle with oil, and scatter some basil leaves on top. Slide the pizza back onto the grill. Cover with the grill lid and grill the pizza until the cheese melts and the bottom of the pizza is crisp and browned, about 2 minutes. There will be leftover sauce. It keeps in the fridge for up to 1 week. It's delicious in Hot Spaghetti Tossed with Raw Tomato Sauce (recipe follows).

Serve the pizzas hot off the grill, allowing them to rest briefly before slicing them into wedges.

HOT SPAGHETTI TOSSED WITH RAW TOMATO SAUCE

Use the juiciest, sweetest, ripe summer tomatoes you can find (maybe you have a garden full of them?—it's everyone's dream) for this light, fresh sauce. Bring a large pot of salted water to a boil over high heat. Add 1 pound spaghetti and cook, stirring occasionally, until the pasta is just cooked through, about 12 minutes. Drain. Toss the pasta with 2–3 cups Raw Tomato Sauce (page 14) in a large bowl. Drizzle with some really good extra-virgin olive oil and season with salt and pepper. Serve with lots of freshly grated parmigiano-reggiano. —— *serves 4–6*

RICE SALAD
serves 4

While regular long-grain rice turns grainy once it spends some time in the refrigerator, short-grain Arborio rice stays tender even when ice-cold. If you do refrigerate the salad, remember to let it come to room temperature before serving to allow the flavors to emerge.

Take a little care to chop the vegetables into even pieces so that everything cooks at the same rate and the salad looks pretty. Feel free to make this salad with whatever you have in the garden or what the season offers at the farmers' market.

½ cup Arborio rice

Salt

1 clove garlic, finely chopped

¼ cup finely chopped pancetta

Handfuls young green beans, coarsely chopped

½ cup shelled peas

½ cup shelled fresh favas, blanched and peeled

Handful sugar snap peas, chopped

2 scallions, trimmed and finely chopped

½ cup grated parmigiano-reggiano or more, to taste

¼ cup really good extra-virgin olive oil

Pepper

Add the rice to a medium pot of salted boiling water over medium-high heat. Add the garlic and pancetta. Cook for about 10 minutes, then add the green beans. Continue cooking, tasting the rice every so often, until the rice is tender, 7–10 minutes. Add the peas and favas during the last few minutes of cooking. Drain the rice and vegetables through a strainer, then transfer to a large mixing bowl. Add the sugar snap peas, scallions, and parmigiano to the hot rice and toss everything together. Add the olive oil and season to taste with salt and pepper. Serve right away or refrigerate. Allow the salad to come to room temperature before serving.

CHICKPEAS TERRA E MARE
serves 6–8

Look for the "Best used by" date when buying a package of chickpeas. The fresher the beans, the more quickly they will cook. Cook a whole pound, it will yield 4–5 cups of beans, more than you'll need for this recipe, so add them to salads or just serve them as a side dish dressed with a little olive oil and lemon.

In Sicily, they sometimes use toasted bread crumbs in place of grated cheese—a holdover from harder times. We just whirl up bread crumbs in a food processor, then transfer to a skillet, toss them with a little olive oil and salt and pepper, and "toast" over medium-high heat until golden. They'll keep in a covered container for up to a week.

1 pound dried chickpeas, or 3–4
  cups canned chickpeas
Salt
½ cup extra-virgin olive oil
1 clove garlic, minced
8 anchovy filets

Pinch of crushed red pepper flakes
3 tablespoons tomato paste
Pepper
Big handful chopped parsley leaves
1 pound orecchiette
1 cup toasted fresh bread crumbs

Put the dried chickpeas in a large pot and cover with water by 4 inches. Cover and bring to a rolling boil over high heat. Turn off the heat and allow the beans to soak undisturbed for about 1 hour. Drain the chickpeas and add fresh water to cover by 2 inches. Bring to a gentle boil over high heat, then reduce the heat to medium-low and cook until the beans are tender. It can take anywhere from 1 to 3 hours, depending on the freshness of the beans. Test them after an hour to see how they are progressing. Add salt, and let them cool in their liquid.

Heat the olive oil in a large pan over medium heat. Add the garlic, anchovies, pepper flakes, and tomato paste. Cook, stirring until the anchovies melt into the oil. Add 3 cups drained chickpeas and stir until everything is well mixed. Season with salt and pepper. Remove from heat and add the chopped parsley.

Meanwhile, cook the orecchiette in a large pot of salted boiling water until just tender, about 10 minutes. Drain (reserve a little pasta water to moisten the sauce if you need to); then return the pasta to the pot. Add the chickpeas and shake the pot carefully to mix everything together. Season with salt and pepper. Serve garnished with the toasted bread crumbs. Serve with lemon wedges, if you like.

contorni

ROASTED ONIONS AGRODOLCE
serves 4–6

We love using the juicy young spring onions that we find in the markets all summer long, but any small sweet onions will do. We roast them in the oven or we grill them when we have the "barbie" fired up, then pour the sweet and sour sauce over the onions and give them a while to marinate.

6 small onions, halved
½ cup extra-virgin olive oil
2 ounces finely chopped pancetta
½ cup brown sugar

½ cup balsamic vinegar, a good quality but not the aged real deal
¼ cup currants
Salt and pepper

Preheat the oven to 400°. Brush the onions with a little of the olive oil and arrange the onion halves, cut side down, in a baking dish. Put the baking dish in the oven.

Heat the remaining olive oil in a small pot over medium heat. Add the pancetta and cook for 5 minutes. Add the sugar and balsamic vinegar, and cook, stirring until the sugar dissolves. Remove from the heat and set aside.

After the onions have cooked for about 30 minutes, remove the baking dish from the oven. Turn the onions cut side up and scatter the currants around the onions. Strain the sauce over the onions, discarding the pancetta. Return the baking dish to the oven and cook until the onions are soft, about 30 minutes.

Remove the baking dish from the oven, season the onions with a little salt and pepper, and set aside to cool. The onions will keep, covered with plastic and refrigerated, for up to 1 week.

GRILLED TOMATOES WITH OLIVE OIL & OREGANO

We make these smoky tomatoes when the charcoal grill is already fired up to medium-hot. Rub 4 large or 6 medium tomatoes with some good extra-virgin olive oil, and slice them in half crosswise. Scoop out the seeds with your finger into a small bowl. Add ½ cup really good extra-virgin olive oil, 1 clove finely minced garlic, 1 small handful chopped fresh oregano leaves, salt, and coarse black pepper, and stir well. Spoon some of the tomato oil into the crannies of the tomatoes. Put the tomatoes cut side up in a metal pan and set the pan on the grill. Close the grill lid and grill the tomatoes until the juices are bubbling and the tomatoes are tender but haven't collapsed, 20–30 minutes. Transfer the tomatoes to a serving platter and spoon more of the tomato oil over them. —— *serves 4–8*

SMALL ZUCCHINI POACHED IN OLIVE OIL

We grow our own zucchini each summer so that we have a constant supply of their golden orange blossoms for frying and stuffing, and so we can pick the squash when they are quite small, often with the flowers still attached. The summer markets in Italy always have these little beauties—our markets here, less so. If you can't find small or "baby" zucchini, choose narrow medium ones and cut them in half or into thirds crosswise. This dish is deliciously plain, so use a very good olive oil because the zucchini become impregnated with it. Poach together 1–2 pounds small zucchini, 2 cloves crushed, peeled garlic, small dried red chile and/or a few sprigs fresh marjoram, and 1–1½ cups really good extra-virgin olive oil in a covered heavy medium pot over low heat until the zucchini are very tender, 15–30 minutes. Serve at room temperature, seasoned with salt, with very fresh mozzarella and crusty bread, if you like. —— *serves 4–8*

TOMATOES WITH TONNATO SAUCE
serves 4–6

We love this sauce so much we spoon it on everything—boiled potatoes, grilled chicken, steamed summer vegetables hot or cold—but our favorite is this beautiful ode to tomato season.

FOR THE TONNATO SAUCE
2 large egg yolks
Salt
Juice of ½ lemon
½ cup canola oil
½ cup really good "smooth & buttery" extra-virgin olive oil
1 small can tuna in olive oil (about 2 ounces), preferably Italian
3 anchovy filets

1 tablespoon capers
1 clove garlic
Pepper

FOR THE TOMATOES
2 pounds tomatoes of various types and sizes, sliced or halved
Arugula leaves
Salt and pepper
Really good extra-virgin olive oil

For the tonnato sauce, whisk together the egg yolks, a pinch of salt, and half of the lemon juice in a medium bowl. Combine both the oils in a measuring cup with a spout. Whisking constantly, add the oil to the yolks, about 1 teaspoon at a time. The sauce will thicken and emulsify. After you've added about ¼ cup of the oil, you can begin to slowly drizzle in the remaining oil as you continue to whisk, until you have a thick glossy mayonnaise. Transfer the sauce to a small bowl.

Purée the tuna, anchovies, capers, and garlic in a food processor until it is smooth. Add a little olive oil to help the process. Use a rubber spatula and press the puréed tuna through a sieve into the mayonnaise. Season to taste with the remaining lemon juice, and salt and pepper. Transfer to a covered container and refrigerate until ready to use. This will keep up to 1 week in the refrigerator.

For the tomatoes, spoon some of the sauce onto individual plates or a platter and arrange the tomatoes on top. Spoon more sauce over the tomatoes and scatter arugula on top. Season with salt and pepper and a drizzle of olive oil.

SWISS CHARD WITH CAPERS & CURRANTS

To make the vinaigrette, purée 6 anchovy filets and 1 clove garlic, along with a pinch of salt to act as grit, in a mortar and pestle. When the purée is smooth, add a pinch of crushed red pepper flakes. Stir in 2 tablespoons red wine vinegar and 2 tablespoons really good extra-virgin olive oil. Add 2 tablespoons capers and 2 tablespoons currants (softened first in a little hot water), then set it aside.

To prepare the Swiss chard, wash 2 pounds Swiss chard well—it is always very sandy. Fold the leaves in half (as you would close a book) and cut out the stems and spines. Trim and finely chop the stems, then chop the leaves. Put the stems in a big colander, strainer, or steamer, and pile the leaves on top. Set it over a large pot filled with 2 inches of water. Bring to a boil over medium-high heat and steam until the stems and leaves are tender, about 10 minutes. Transfer to a large bowl and pour the vinaigrette over the warm chard. Set aside and allow to cool. To form the chard, fill a small mold or a half-cup metal measuring cup with chard, and press firmly. Unmold onto a platter, and continue making molds with the rest of the chard. Spoon any remaining vinaigrette over everything. —— *serves 4*

ROMANO BEANS STEWED IN TOMATO SAUCE

We've both had terrific luck growing the large, flat, green Romano bean in our gardens at home. Every spring we plant the "magic" seeds and by midsummer the stalks are so tall and vigorous, it seems they could indeed keep growing clear up to the sky; a stepladder is the only way to reach the beans at the top. These are stewing beans—they need to simmer for a time to become tender—and we like ours soft.

Put 1 pound Romano beans, 2–3 cloves crushed, peeled garlic, 4 cups passata di pomodoro or strained tomatoes, ¼–½ cup extra-virgin olive oil, 2 sprigs fresh basil, ½ cup water, and salt and pepper to taste into a heavy, medium, nonreactive pot with a tight-fitting lid. Bring to a simmer over medium heat. Reduce the heat and gently simmer the beans in the sauce, stirring occasionally, until they are very tender, 45–60 minutes. Adjust seasonings. Serve the beans with lots of the flavorful sauce. —— *serves 6*

Pesce

MIXED SEAFOOD GRILL WITH SALMORIGLIO
serves 4–8

We fancy octopus for its sweet, tender, meaty flesh. Most octopus sold in the United States is available frozen—a good thing because freezing helps tenderize it. Cooking it in gently simmering water keeps it from becoming tough. Finishing it on the grill adds the smoky flavor of summer.

For the mixed grill
1 cup white wine vinegar
One 5–6 pound octopus, cleaned
12–16 large unpeeled shrimp
6 large squid, cleaned
Extra-virgin olive oil
Salt
2 pinches crushed red pepper flakes
2–3 lemons, halved

For the salmoriglio
Juice of 2 lemons
1–2 cloves garlic, minced
Small handful fresh oregano leaves, chopped
Small handful fresh parsley leaves, chopped
1 cup extra-virgin olive oil
Salt and pepper

For the mixed grill, bring a large pot of water to a boil over high heat. Add the vinegar and the octopus and reduce the heat to low. Cover and very gently simmer until the rest of the octopus is tender, 1–1½ hours. Drain and set aside until cool enough to handle. Cut off the head and cut out the hard "beak" in the center, leaving the rest of the octopus intact. Peel off the skin, if you like. Put the octopus into a large pan along with the shrimp and squid. Drizzle with olive oil and season with salt and pepper flakes.

For the salmoriglio, put the lemon juice, garlic, oregano, and parsley into a medium bowl and stir in the olive oil. Season with salt and pepper.

Prepare a hot to medium-hot fire to one side of a charcoal or gas grill. Grill the octopus, shrimp, and squid over the hotter section of coals until well marked and slightly charred in places, about 5 minutes. Move the seafood to a cooler spot on the grill if there are flare-ups. The squid should be opaque, the shrimp just cooked through, and the octopus just needs a little color and smoke. Arrange the seafood and lemons on a large serving platter. Serve with a bowl of salmoriglio to spoon over the seafood.

COLD POACHED SEA BASS &
LEMON-ANCHOVY MAYONNAISE
serves 4–6

When the weather turns hot and muggy and takes our appetites away, we prepare this simple *in bianco* dish. The mayonnaise alone restores our hunger for more.

FOR THE POACHED FISH
Salt
One 2-pound sea bass filet or other
firm white-fleshed fish filet

FOR THE MAYONNAISE
6–8 anchovy filets
Grated zest and juice of 2 lemons
2 cups mayonnaise

For the poached fish, fill a deep medium pan with water and season it with a few generous pinches of salt to make it nearly as salty as the sea. Put the fish into the water and bring to a gentle simmer over medium heat. Adjust the heat to keep the water barely bubbling.

Poach the fish until it is just opaque in the center (8–10 minutes per inch at its thickest point). Transfer the fish with a slotted spatula to a paper towel–lined plate to drain. When the fish has cooled off, cover it with plastic wrap and refrigerate until well chilled, 2–4 hours.

For the mayonnaise, crush the anchovies to a paste using a large mortar and pestle, or finely chop them and transfer to a medium bowl. Stir in the lemon zest and juices. Add the mayonnaise, stirring until smooth. This makes about 2¼ cups. The mayonnaise keeps in the refrigerator for up to 1 week.

Serve the fish with a generous spoonful of mayonnaise on each plate.

SALMON CARPACCIO ALLA HARRY'S BAR
serves 4–6

Freezing the well-wrapped salmon for a couple of hours firms up the flesh and makes slicing easier. This sauce is a version of the one they serve over thinly sliced raw beef at the famed Harry's Bar in Venice. But we love to make it with wild Pacific salmon instead of meat.

FOR THE MAIONESE SAUCE
1 large egg yolk
Salt
Juice of ½ lemon
½ cup canola oil
½ cup really good "smooth &
  buttery" extra-virgin olive oil
2 teaspoons Worcestershire sauce

3–5 tablespoons milk
White pepper
1 tablespoon fresh tarragon leaves,
  finely chopped

FOR THE SALMON
1 pound center-cut salmon filet, skin
  and pinbones removed

For the maionese sauce, whisk together the egg yolk, a pinch of salt, and half of the lemon juice in a medium bowl. Combine both the oils in a measuring cup with a spout. Whisking constantly, add the oil to the yolk about 1 teaspoon at a time. The sauce will thicken and emulsify. After you've added about ¼ cup of the oil, you can begin to slowly drizzle in the remaining oil as you continue to whisk, until you have a thick, glossy maionese. Add more of the remaining lemon juice to season the sauce, if you like. Stir in the Worcestershire sauce and the milk, then season to taste with salt and pepper. Transfer to a covered container and refrigerate until ready to use. The sauce will keep for up to 1 week in the refrigerator. Mix in the tarragon just before using.

For the salmon, use a long-blade knife to cut the salmon across the grain into very thin slices. Evenly divide the sliced salmon between 4–6 dinner plates, arranging the slices in a mosaic pattern. Place pieces of plastic wrap over the salmon, and using a flat meat-pounder or even a metal measuring cup with a flat bottom, press down on the plastic, until the salmon spreads out and covers the whole plate. Repeat with all the plates of salmon. You can stack the plates and refrigerate them until you are ready to sauce and serve them.

Remove and discard the plastic wrap. Use a dinner fork to beat the sauce and thin it with a little more milk if it's too thick. Drizzle the sauce over the salmon in free-form "Jackson Pollock" fashion. Serve cold.

Carne

GRILLED STEAK WITH BOTTARGA BUTTER
serves 6–8

We pay homage to the famous Tuscan *bistecca alla fiorentina* with a nice, fat, dry-aged porterhouse and grill it over hardwood charcoal until it's charred on the outside and quite rare inside. The Italians may think we've lost our minds, but we like to anoint our steak with flavored butter, in this case with shaved bottarga, the dried roe of tuna or gray mullet that is a specialty of Sicilian and Sardinian cooking—our idea of a summer surf 'n' turf platter.

1 porterhouse steak, 2–3 inches thick
Salt and pepper
8 tablespoons (1 stick) softened butter

1 ounce bottarga, finely grated
Finely grated zest of 1 lemon

Prepare a hot charcoal or gas grill. Meanwhile, season both sides of the steak with salt and pepper, and set aside.

Beat the butter in a bowl with a wooden spoon to make it smooth and a bit creamy. Add the bottarga and lemon zest, and season with pepper. Stir to combine. The butter can be used right away, or covered and refrigerated for up to 3 days.

Grill the steak over the hottest section of coals until a good browned crust has developed on the first side, about 8 minutes. To ensure a good crust, resist the urge to move or fiddle with the steak while it's cooking, but if flare-ups threaten to burn the meat, you've got to move it to a cooler spot on the grill. Turn the steak and grill the second side for 5 minutes.

Move the steak to a cooler spot on the grill to finish cooking it, turning occasionally, until the internal temperatures reach 120° for rare, 130° for medium-rare, and 140° for medium, 5–15 minutes longer depending on the thickness of the steak and the desired doneness.

Pull the steak off the grill and let it rest for 10 minutes. Slather it with some of the bottarga butter. Cut the steak from the bone and slice the meat. Serve the meat, and the bone goes to one lucky dog!

ROLLED FLANK STEAK WITH PESTO
serves 6

We use green olives stuffed with anchovies in this pesto. We first had these delicacies at the bar at Le Caprice in London, where we were laying over on our way to Rome. They are a great salty nibble with a drink so we always keep them on hand. If you can find them, then use them and leave out the anchovies, unless you are anchovy-mad like we are. You can grill the steak ahead and serve it cold with a big salad. Simple summer-style entertaining—that way you can take a swim, or run through the sprinkler before dinner.

FOR THE PESTO
2 loosely packed cups basil leaves
2 loosely packed cups Italian parsley leaves
1 clove garlic, sliced
¼–½ cup pitted green olives
3 anchovy filets

¼ cup really good extra-virgin olive oil
½ cup parmigiano-reggiano

FOR THE STEAK
One 2-pound flank steak
Salt and pepper

For the pesto, purée the basil, parsley, garlic, green olives, anchovies, with the olive oil in a food processor. Add the parmigiano and pulse a couple of times. Transfer to a small bowl and place a piece of plastic wrap directly on the surface of the pesto to keep the sauce from turning dark.

For the steak, place the flank steak flat on a work surface with the grain of the meat running perpendicular to you. Using a long, thin, very sharp knife, butterfly the meat by slicing through the long side of the steak, opening it up as you go, stopping ½ inch short of cutting the steak in two. Press the meat flat. Spread the pesto all over the meat, leaving a 1-inch space all around. Roll up the steak, with the grain running the length of the roll (this is the way it "wants" to roll) and tie up with kitchen string every 2 inches. Wrap with plastic wrap and refrigerate until ready to grill.

Grill over a medium-hot fire built on one side of the grill, turning the steak until it has browned on all sides, about 10 minutes. Move the steak over to the side of the grill off the fire, allowing it to cook as it rests, about 10 minutes.

Place the steak on a cutting board and allow to rest for 10 minutes. Remove the strings and slice across the grain into 1 to 2-inch slices.

A PILE OF GRILLED LAMB CHOPS SCOTTADITO
serves 4

Scottadito is loosely translated as "finger-blistering hot". So we dispense with a knife and fork as they do in Rome, just pick them up, and nibble away. We sometimes serve these as a first course. Not only are they delicious, but they are a real icebreaker. It is hard to be reticent when you are licking your fingers!

1 clove garlic	Juice of ½ lemon
Salt	12 rib lamb chops
1–2 tablespoons harissa	1 lemon, quartered
¼ cup extra-virgin olive oil	Pepper

Smash and mash the garlic with a big pinch of salt (to add a little grit) in a mortar and pestle to make a smooth paste. Stir in the harissa, olive oil, and lemon juice.

Use a flat-bottomed meat pounder to press down and flatten the meat of the chop. Arrange the chops in a large baking pan, brushing both sides with the marinade. Cover with plastic wrap and set aside for about an hour, or refrigerate for about 4 hours.

Grill the chops over a medium-hot fire until beautifully browned, about 3 minutes per side. Or preheat a large seasoned cast-iron or nonstick skillet over medium-high heat. The skillet is ready when a little water flicked into the pan sizzles and evaporates right away. Add the chops and cooked until crispy and brown, 2–3 minutes, then flip them over and cook for 2–3 minutes. Pile the chops on a big platter along with the lemon wedges, season with salt and pepper, and let everyone eat them with their fingers! But remember, they're "finger-blistering hot"!

FRIED RABBIT & FRITTO MISTO OF HERBS
serves 4

We are lucky enough to have a young couple nearby who raise livestock in the old-fashioned humane way—including, just recently, rabbit. Yes, the delicate white meat many Americans are squeamish about. But, it *is* delicious. In summer, we serve it fried—hot or cold, as you would fried chicken—alongside a fritto misto of the herbs rabbits like to eat.

FOR THE FRITTO MISTO
½ cup all-purpose flour
¼ teaspoon salt
½–1 cup white wine
2 handfuls fresh sage leaves
2 handfuls fresh parsley sprigs
Canola oil

FOR THE RABBIT
2 cups all-purpose flour
3 eggs
Olive oil
1 cleaned rabbit, cut into 12 pieces
Salt and pepper
Capers, drained
1–2 lemons, quartered

For the fritto misto, whisk the flour and salt together in a medium bowl. Gradually add the wine, whisking until smooth. Let the batter rest for 30 minutes.

For the rabbit, put the flour in a dish, beat the eggs in another dish, and set both aside. Add enough olive oil to a large heavy skillet to reach a depth of ½ inch. Heat over medium heat until hot but not smoking (or until it reaches 350° on a candy thermometer).

Meanwhile, season the rabbit with salt and pepper. Dredge each piece in flour, dip in egg, then dredge in flour again, shaking off the excess. Working in batches, fry the rabbit until golden brown all over, about 10 minutes. Use tongs to transfer the rabbit to a wire rack set over paper towels to drain. Season with a little salt while still hot.

To fry the herbs, add enough canola oil to a deep heavy pot to reach a depth of 2 inches. Heat the oil over medium heat until hot or until it reaches 350° on a candy thermometer. Give the batter a quick whisk.

Dip 1 sage leaf or parsley sprig at a time in the batter and carefully lower it into the hot oil. Fry the herbs in small batches until golden and crisp, about 1 minute. Drain on a wire rack. Season with salt while still hot. Serve the rabbit and herbs scattered with capers and garnished with lemon.

Finale

FIG GELATO
makes 1 quart

We have several fledgling fig trees that bear beautiful leaves and, if we're lucky, a handful of fruit. Fig country we do not live in! But we adore the sweet jammy fruit and use preserves to make this exquisite gelato. When we eat it, we like to close our eyes and pretend the rich fig flavor came from our very own figs on our very own trees.

2 cups whole milk	Pinch of salt
1 cup heavy cream	1 cup fig preserves
¾ cup sugar	2 teaspoons vanilla bean paste or
6 egg yolks	vanilla extract

Put the milk, cream, and ½ cup of the sugar into a heavy saucepan and bring to a simmer over medium heat, stirring gently until the sugar dissolves.

Meanwhile, put the yolks, salt, and the remaining ¼ cup of sugar into a medium mixing bowl and whisk together until the yolks are thick and pale yellow.

Gradually ladle about 1 cup of the hot milk into the yolks, whisking constantly. Stir the warm yolk mixture into the hot milk in the saucepan. Reduce the heat to low and cook, stirring constantly, until the custard is thick enough to coat the back of the spoon and registers between 175° and 180° on an instant-read thermometer, about 10 minutes. Stirring the custard constantly as it cooks and thickens helps prevent it from coming to a boil and curdling.

Strain the custard into a medium bowl. Stir in the fig preserves and the vanilla. Set the bowl into a larger bowl filled with ice, then stir the custard frequently until it has cooled. Cover the custard and refrigerate it until completely chilled, about 4 hours (though it can keep in the refrigerator for up to 2 days).

Churn the custard in an ice cream maker following the manufacturer's directions. Scoop the gelato (it will have the consistency of soft-serve) into a quart container with a lid, cover, and freeze for a couple of hours until it is just firm. The gelato will keep for up to 3 days in the freezer.

CHILLED STRAWBERRIES & MOSCATO D'ASTI

When we find sweet summer strawberries at the market, we like to soak them in this pretty sparkling dessert wine from Italy's Piedmont, and serve them for dessert on hot evenings. Put 1 pint hulled strawberries into a medium bowl, halving or quartering any large berries. Sprinkle them with 2 tablespoons sugar, adding more or less, depending on your taste and how sweet the berries are. Pour 1 cup Moscato d'Asti over the berries and stir gently. Put the strawberries in the refrigerator to macerate for 2–3 hours. Serve in pretty dessert dishes with the wine spooned over the berries. —*serves 2–4*

SWEET RICOTTA & SHAVED CHOCOLATE

This simple dessert relies on very fresh, creamy ricotta, which any good Italian market carries, and really good chocolate. Stir 2 tablespoons sugar into 2 cups really good, fresh ricotta. Spoon the ricotta into 4–6 pretty little dessert dishes and refrigerate. It should be served nice and cold. Just before serving, shave 2–3 ounces best quality semisweet or dark chocolate on the large holes of a box grater over the ricotta, showering each dish with a pile of chocolate shavings. —*serves 4–6*

The table awaits at Trattoria Coco Lezzone in Florence.